SNOOPY
LOVES to DOODLE

Create and complete pictures with Snoopy and friends
BY CHARLES M. SCHULZ

RP|KIDS
PHILADELPHIA • LONDON

ISBN 978-0-7624-4378-9
Library of Congress Control Number: 2011927754

9 8 7 6 5 4 3 2 1
Digit on the right indicates the number of this printing

Art adapted by Ryan Hayes
Cover and interior design by Ryan Hayes
Edited by Lisa Cheng
Typography: Typography of Coop

Published by Running Press Kids
an imprint of Running Press Book Publishers
A Member of the Perseus Books Group
2300 Chestnut Street
Philadelphia, PA 19103–4371

Visit us on the web!
www.runningpress.com

Who is the subject of Snoopy's
latest masterpiece?

The Red Baron wants to know what's for dinner.
Fill the table with your favorite foods.

Give Spike a scenic place to picnic! Fill the desert
around him with cacti, rocks, and plants.

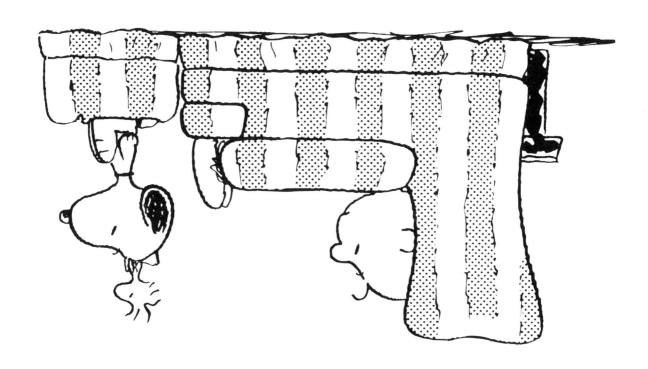

What friends are watching TV with Charlie Brown, Snoopy, and Woodstock?

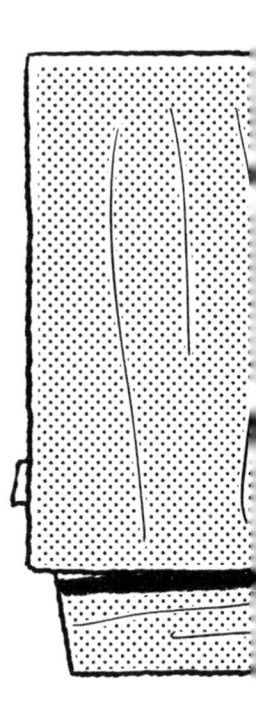

Off to sea! Decorate the sail and
flag of Woodstock's boat.

Give Snoopy something fun to play with,
like a tennis racquet and a ball.

It's Woodstock's family tree! Help fill in the branches with Woodstock's feathered relatives.

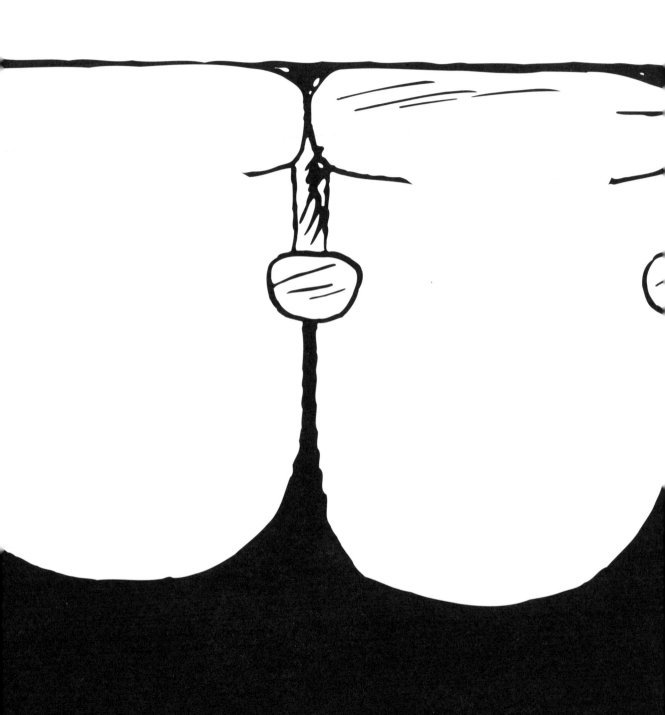

Who is at the movies with Snoopy?

Poor Woodstock is all alone!
Draw some friends for his empty nest.

Snoopy's team is the winner!
Award them a shiny trophy.

What is Linus throwing
for Snoopy to catch?

Cowabunga! Draw Snoopy
a snowboard.

Draw lots of fluffy flakes for Snoopy to catch on his tongue. Remember, no two snowflakes are the same!

What kinds of ice cream cones are
Snoopy and Woodstock enjoying?

What is Snoopy ready to catch?

Where did that golf ball go?
And did Snoopy sink a hole in one?

Who are driving the other Zambonis?

Decorate the flags that Woodstock and Snoopy
are waving proudly.

What does Snoopy see on his
drive through the country?

Snoopy rides his motorcycle through city streets.
Draw a skyline behind him.

Fall is in the air! Draw piles of leaves for
Snoopy and Woodstock to jump into.

Show your troop pride!
What do the scouts' flags look like?

What flag does this fearless leader wave?

Will Snoopy use a raft or a bridge
to rescue Woodstock? You decide!

Draw some lampshade hats
for Woodstock's friends.

Draw a snowman for Snoopy
to hang the top hat on.

Make a wish! Finish the field of dandelions.

Happy Holidays! Help Spike decorate
the cactus for the season.

All aboard the SS Snoopy!
Draw a boat for this canine captain.

Decorate Snoopy's sailboat
as he sets out to sea!

Yum! What sort of food
has chef Snoopy cooked?

Draw some trees and flowers
that Snoopy has planted.

What sights will Woodstock see
as he flies high in the sky?

What kind of treasure has Snoopy
and his pirate gang discovered?

What is Snoopy watering in his garden?

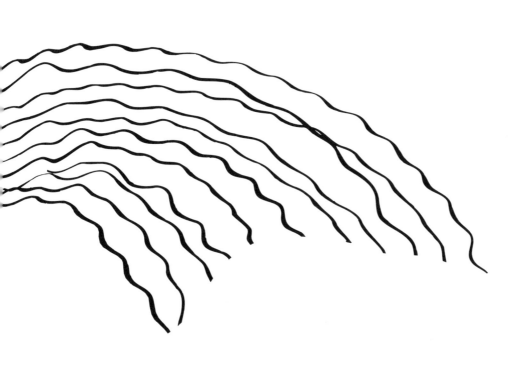

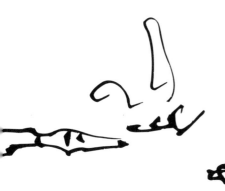

Draw a boat so Spike can set sail!

Snoopy's catching a wave!
Draw in some waves for Snoopy to ride.

Help Charlie Brown and Snoopy
decorate the tree.

What kinds of camping supplies
did Snoopy pack in his bag?

Help Snoopy find water for his campers.

Do Snoopy, Woodstock, and their friends see wild animals on the hike?

Make sure that Woodstock and his friends have all
the gear they need for their camping trip.

What does Snoopy see
when he is in outer space?

What piece of artwork
is Joe Cool showing off?

Are the fish biting for Woodstock and Snoopy?

Snoopy needs a piano to lean against
and music in the air. Help him out!

What kind of ball is Snoopy kicking?

What is Charlie Brown holding
that makes Snoopy so happy?

How did Snoopy carve his Jack O' Lantern?

Draw Woodstock's musical instrument.

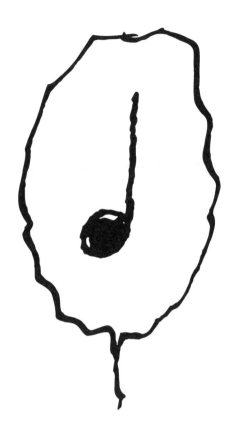

What is Snoopy looking at
from the top of his dog house?

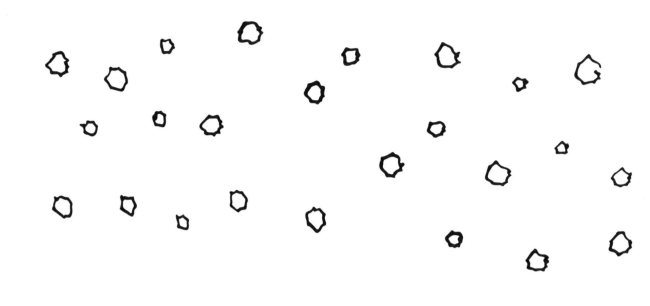

Let it snow! Finish this wintry scene.

Snoopy is practicing his poker face!
Who is he playing with?

Make sure that there is a football
for Snoopy to catch!